Making Costume Jewelry

An Easy & Complete Step By Step Guide

Title: Making Costume Jewelry

Author Name: Janet Evans

Copyright © 2012
http://ultimatehowtoguides.com

All rights reserved.

No part of this publication may be copied, reproduced in any format, by any means, electronic or otherwise, without prior consent from the copyright owner and publisher of this book.

Table of Contents

Introduction 7

Chapter 1 – Tools Needed For Making Costume Jewelry .. 9
- Tool 1 – Round Nose Pliers 9
- Tool 2 – Flat Nose or Chain Nose Pliers 9
- Tool 3 – Wire or Side Cutters 10
- Tool 4 – Crimping Pliers 11
- Tool 5 – Awl 11
- Tool 6 – Hammer 12
- Tool 7 – Scissors 12
- Tool 8 – Tweezers 12
- Tool 9 – Measuring Stick and Measuring Tape 13
- Tool 10 – Bead Board 13
- Tool 11 – Beading Needles 14
- Tool 12 – Adhesives 14
- Tool 13 – Wire Jig 15

Chapter 2 – Materials Needed For Making Costume Jewelry 16
- Material 1 – Jewelry Wire 16
  - Wire 1 – Dead Soft 16
  - Wire 2 – Half Hard 17
  - Wire 3 – Full Hard 17
  - Copper Wire 17
  - Plated Wire 18
  - Artistic Wire 18
  - Galvanized Wire 18
  - Sterling Silver Wire 18
  - Fine Silver Wire 19
  - Gold Filled Wire 19
  - Gold Wire 19
  - Memory Wire 19
  - French Wire 19
- Material 2 – Beadalon 20
- Material 3 – Cord And Thread 21
  - Elastic Cord 21
  - Invisible Cord 21

- Kevlar 22
- Leather Cord 22
- Nymo 22
- Nylon Thread 22
- Polyester Cord 23
- Satin Cord 23
- Silamide 23
- Silk Thread 23
- Suede Cord 23

Material 4 – Beads 24
- Acrylic Beads 24
- Swarovski Beads and Crystals 25
- Semi Precious Gemstone Beads 25
- Glass Beads 25
- Metal Beads 25
- Seed Beads 26
- Shamballa Fashion Beads 26
- Wood Beads 26

Material 5 – Jewelry Clasps 26
- Adjustable Clasp 27
- Ball And Joint Clasp 27
- Bar And Ring Toggle Clasp 28
- Barrel Clasp 28
- Bead Clasp 29
- Box Clasp 29
- Button Toggle Clasp 30
- Crimping Clasp 30
- Filigree Clasp 30
- Fishhook Clasp 30
- Hook And Eye Clasp 31
- Lobster Claw Clasp 31
- Magnetic Clasp 32
- Multi Strand Clasp 32
- S Hook Clasp 33
- Screw Clasp 33
- Slide Lock Clasp 34
- Snap Lock Clasp 34
- Springing Clasp 35
- Swivel Clasp 35
- Tab Lock Clasp 36
- Twister Clasp 36

Material 6 – Jewelry Findings 37
   Crimp Tube And Cover 37
   Jump Ring 38
   Head Pin And Eye Pin 38
   Bead Tips 39
   Jewelry Links 39
   Bails 40
   Bead Cap 40
   Cones 41
   Bead Frame 41

Chapter 3 – Where To Buy Equipment And Materials For Making Costume Jewelry 43
   Place 1 – Hobby And Craft Store 43
   Place 2 – eBay 43
   Place 3 – Online Jewelry Supply Stores 44
   How To Go About Purchasing Material And Equipment For Making Costume Jewelry On A Budget 44
   Types Of Costume Jewelry 46
      Type 1 – Vintage Costume Jewelry 46
      Type 2 – Reproduction Costume Jewelry 46
      Type 3 – Normal Costume Jewelry 47

Chapter 4 – Tips To Get Started Making Costume Jewelry 48
   Finding Inspiration For Making Costume Jewelry 50
   Tips To Help With Making Costume Jewelry A Lot Easier 52

Chapter 5 – Some Projects For Making Costume Jewelry You May Want To Try 54
   Project 1 – Lampwork Bracelet 56
      Supplies Required To Make Lampwork Bracelet 56
   Project 2 – Amethyst Link Bracelet 60
      Supplies Required To Make Amethyst Link Bracelet 60
   Project 3 – Watermelon Tourmaline Bracelet 62
      Supplies Needed For Making Watermelon Tourmaline Bracelet 62
   Project 4 – Chain Drop Earrings 63
      Supplies Needed For Making Chain Drop Earrings 64
   Project 5 – Winter White Pearl & Glass Earrings 66
      Supplies Needed To Make Winter White Pearl & Glass Earrings 66

Project 6 – Chunky Lava Bread Wire Wrapped Pendant & Chain 68
   Supplies Needed For Making Chunky Lava Bread Wire Wrapped Pendant & Chain 68
Project 7 – Chunky Funky Heart Necklace 72
   Supplies Needed To Make The Chunky Funky Heart Necklace 72
Project 8 – Kokopelli Pendant With Glass & Turquoise Beads Necklace.. 75
   Supplies You Need For Making Kokopelli Pendant With Glass & Turquoise Beads 76

Introduction

If you're someone who has an eye for fashion and enjoys making their own things, why not save yourself money by making your own costume jewelry. Even the simplest pieces of costume jewelry can be overpriced so why spend money on such accessories when making them for yourself could save you a great deal of money.

Of course when it comes to making your own jewelry there are certain things you need to consider before you do.

The first thing you need to consider before you begin the process of learning how to make costume jewelry is what type you wish to make. The best way of determining what style of jewelry you want to make is to look through various magazines and see what's on offer in stores locally. It's also a good idea to gain inspiration for your costume jewelry designs by visiting museums or art galleries. You may even gain inspiration for your designs when out for a walk.

It's a good idea as you go through various magazines, newspapers or when you look online you keep copies of images of costume jewelry that you like. Then look at these images to help you to come up with your own unique designs.

In this book we offer help about how to go about making costume jewelry including some projects you may want to try. However if you can, see whether there are any jewelry making classes close to where you live. Of course if you cannot find any locally then there are plenty of classes to be found online as well.

Another thing you should be doing is to designate a particular area in your home where you'll work on your jewelry pieces. It's important to remember, even when making the simplest of pieces you'll require lots of different items to complete the project. Plus you need plenty of space to be able to work on each piece of jewelry comfortably.

If you have a small room in your home that's used for storing things in then this would be the perfect place for setting up as your jewelry workspace. It's a good idea to spend money not only investing in the tools you need to create your designs with but also a good table and chair. You want the space where you're sitting to be comfortable and also allow you to not place too much stress on your body as you do work.

Remember you're going to be working with very small items so make sure the area in which you are working is well lit. If you need to purchase a good standard lamp or reading lamp that can direct light straight on to the work surface from above. Also investing in a light that contains LED bulbs rather than conventional incandescent or halogen bulbs should be considered. This is because these types of lights actually produce a form of lighting that's very similar to natural sunlight, so it means far less strain is being placed on your eyes as you work on very small and delicate parts of the jewelry.

As for the chair, make sure you choose one that offers your back plenty of support. So investing in a good quality typist's type chair should be considered. Not only do they provide support to the upper part of the back but also the lower part.

Also make sure you look for a store that can reliably provide you with all the materials you need when making costume jewelry. If you're having problems sourcing what you need locally there are plenty of online stores you can use instead.

Chapter 1 – Tools Needed For Making Costume Jewelry

When it comes to buying the tools needed for making costume jewelry you'll find there is a huge selection to choose from. However what's important is when investing money in such items buy the best quality ones you can afford. Not only will these tools last considerably longer, but will help to ensure the whole process of making jewelry pieces is a lot easier.

The types of tools you'll need to buy when it comes to making any type of costume jewelry are as follows.

Tool 1 – Round Nose Pliers

It's with these pliers you are going to find bending the wire and making loops a lot easier. Of all the tools you will invest in for making any jewelry even the costume type, you'll find this is the tool you'll be using the most often. It's important that the round nose pliers you purchase aren't the standard DIY kind but those specifically designed for making jewelry, as they are much smaller.

Tool 2 – Flat Nose or Chain Nose Pliers

These are useful in many different ways, not only will use these pliers to hold your pieces as you work on them but also for when you need to open or close jump rings or links in a chain. Although these two pliers may do pretty much the same job if you need to get into tight spaces. In fact if you cannot decide which pair you should be investing in, I would highly recommend initially you get a pair of chain nose pliers and then invest in the flat nose ones once your ability begins to improve.

Tool 3 – Wire or Side Cutters

Without a pair of these you won't be able to cut the wire or other materials you use for stringing your jewelry designs together. However if you're going to be using memory wire to make costume jewelry then investing in a good pair of memory wire cutters is essential.

Tool 4 – Crimping Pliers

This particular tool is the one you use to crimp beads and which helps to ensure the beads will stay securely in position. It also helps to ensure the rest of the beads and other ornaments used in your design remain in place as well.

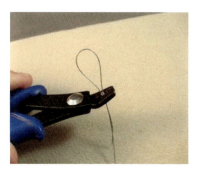

Tool 5 – Awl

You'll need this tool if you intend to do any kind of knotting when making costume jewelry. Without an awl you'll find it very difficult to produce knots that are not only of the same size and shape but also are very tight.

Tool 6 – Hammer

You don't need a very big hammer just one that will allow you to flatten wire out so it becomes much harder and will in turn help to ensure it keeps its shape much better.

Tool 7 – Scissors

A really good pair of short sharp scissors is crucial when it comes to wanting to make any sort of jewelry. A sharp pair of scissors will ensure that when cutting materials such as leather, suede, silk or satin the ends don't become frayed.

Tool 8 – Tweezers

Yes these are the same tool you would use to pluck your eyebrows at home. A good pair of tweezers proves invaluable when you want to pick up very tiny beads to then thread on to the wire or other stringing material. By holding the beads between the tweezers you can then hold them up to the light and see exactly where the hole is through which the wire or other stringing material needs to be threaded.

Tool 9 – Measuring Stick and Measuring Tape

You may be wondering why we recommend you get a measuring stick when you already have a measuring scale on your bead board. The measuring stick will be used to ensure you cut the right length of wire or material for making customer jewelry with. Whilst the measuring tape is crucial to making sure you know exactly what circumference a person's neck or wrist is whom you're making jewelry for.

Tool 10 – Bead Board

As well as having compartments in which various size beads can be stored, this particular piece of equipment also comes with a measuring scale and a groove into which the beads can

13

be placed. Investing in such equipment means not only are the beads close to hand when needed but you can immediately which size they are.

Tool 11 – Beading Needles

This is a crucial piece of equipment you need to buy, as you'll find threading small or tiny beads on to thin thread can prove difficult. It is best if you invest money in several different size needles.

Tool 12 – Adhesives

You may be wondering why you need adhesive to make costume jewelry with. You'll need to invest money in two forms of adhesive for making costume jewelry with. You'll need a resin based ones that allows you to adhere china and glass to metal. Plus you need to invest in a strong clear all purpose adhesive for when you want to stick wooden beads for example on to materials such as leather or other fabric types.

Tool 13 – Wire Jig

When it comes to working with wire you may find using pliers alone difficult and that's why buying a wire jig should be considered. These jigs (boards) tend to be made from aluminium, wood or some transparent plastic material in which small holes have been drilled. You can then place pins into the holes, which then allow you to bend the wire around them to make your own designs.

Of course if you'd rather save money, you may want to consider making your own wire jig instead. To do this you will need a block of wood and some very small nails. Now you need to drill into the wood numerous holes into which the nails can then be inserted. It's important you make the holes large enough for the nails to fit into them snuggly, as you don't want them moving around as you work the wire around.

Chapter 2 – Materials Needed For Making Costume Jewelry

As you'll soon discover when it comes to making costume jewelry there are many different materials you can use. Of course you could use expensive materials such as crystals, gold or silver charms. However why not consider using less expensive materials to create some very unique and stunning pieces of costume jewelry as well.

Now we'll go into a little more detail regarding the kinds of materials you can.

Material 1 – Jewelry Wire

When you want to make your own costume jewelry the first thing you need to buy is a wide selection of different types of jewelry wire. This is because the wire available may be more suitable for certain jewelry items than others.

To make sure you buy the right types I'll explain what they are.

Wire 1 – Dead Soft

16

Of all the types of jewelry wire you can buy this is the most flexible, meaning it can be manipulated in a number of different ways to form some amazing designs. This really is the best wire to use when you want to include wrapped wire or sculpted designs with your pieces of jewelry.

Wire 2 – Half Hard

This is slightly harder than the dead soft type of jewelry wire you can buy, but is still flexible enough it can be bent using your hands. The big benefit to including this type of wire into a piece of jewelry is it holds its shape far better than the dead soft jewelry wire does. This type of wire is perfect for any piece of jewelry you're designing and then making.

Wire 3 – Full Hard

This type of jewelry wire is extremely stiff and if you're try to shape it using your hands you'd find it extremely difficult as it's not flexible at all. I would recommend you use this type of wire when making drop earrings.

However when it comes to making custom jewelry you don't have to just consider how soft or hard the wire is but what it's actually made from. Again you're going to find there are many different types of wire to select from and below we briefly explain just what these are.

Copper Wire

This is the cheapest type of wire you can buy for making jewelry with. I would highly recommend you purchase this when you are learning how to make your own pieces of jewelry initially.

Plated Wire

The problem with this is that the gold or silver coating on this wire will eventually wear off and when used in making jewelry can make the piece look tacky after a while. Again I would suggest you use this wire only when you're practicing making a particular piece of custom jewelry you've designed yourself. Then if anything goes wrong it won't cost a fortune.

Artistic Wire

The benefit to using this wire is that it comes in a huge array of colors so finding one to complement the rest of your design shouldn't prove a problem. This type of wire comes with either a very high metallic shine to it or a matte finish. The way in which the enamel has been applied ensures that when working with it, the coating will not chip, peel or become tarnished even if heat is applied to it.

Galvanized Wire

This is dull silver in color and is something your local DIY or hardware store will stock. Again like the copper wire and plated wire this is the kind you should be using to practice making certain designs with.

Sterling Silver Wire

It's important to check this wires purity. The best type of sterling silver wire should contain 92.5% pure silver. This is one of the most popular types of wires. Not only is it very flexible; allowing you to bend and coil it in to a variety of different shapes it can also be hammered flat easily as well.

The reason why the use of sterling silver wire is so popular when making costume jewelry is not only is it very durable, but also very economical to buy. Plus, when you attach any other items to it, you can create some fabulous looking pieces of jewelry.

Fine Silver Wire

This particular wire is made from 99.9% pure silver and is a great deal softer than sterling silver. Although it means it's even more flexible, getting it to hold a particular form does prove a lot harder.

Gold Filled Wire

This type of wire is normally made from a base metal such as copper, silver or brass over which a very thin coating of gold has been laid. The main benefit of using such wire in your designs is it costs a great deal less than real gold wire and you'll find it a lot easier to handle.

Gold Wire

Yes it does make any piece of costume jewelry look wonderful, but of course is the most expensive type of jewelry wire you can buy.

Memory Wire

This type of wire is made in such a way that it is easy to handle yet also will retain the shapes it's formed into. It comes in a variety of different weights and when using much larger beads, or items on your costume jewelry then use the heaviest weight memory wire you can.

French Wire

You may find some places where you can buy this wire from, refer to it as bullion or gimp. Often this type of wire is very thin and is the kind you should be using to conceal the wire you've threaded through clasps or crimps. As well as helping to strengthen and protect the ends of your jewelry pieces it also helps to ensure a more professional look to the jewelry once it's been finished.

Another thing you also need to think about when buying wire is what size you should be using. As you'll discover it comes in a variety of different sizes. What size you need, will depend on what item of jewelry you're going to make.

Earrings and Earring Wires – 20g (0.8mm) or 22g (0.6mm) Wire
Clasps and Hooks – 18g (1.0mm) or 20g (0.8mm) Wire
Single Loops For Bracelets and Necklaces - 18g (1.0mm) or 20g (0.8mm) Wire
Wrapped Loops In Bracelets and Necklaces – 20g(0.8mm) to 24g (0.5mm) Wire
Spirals – 17g (1.2mm) to 20g (0.8mm) Wire
Jump Rings – 18g (1.0mm) to 20g (0.8mm) Wire

Material 2 – Beadalon

This is another material you can use and is in fact made up of tiny wires, which have been twisted together and then been coated in nylon. How flexible it is will depend on how many wires have been twisted together. Be aware however, that the more strands of wire used in the making of this material actually help to make it much more flexible.

Therefore, if you want to make sure you can form shapes easily, then you would be best using Beadalon that's comprised of 49 twisted strands of wire rather than made up of 7 or 19. However if you want the Beadalon to hold its shape better you'll need to go for the type that comprises less strands in it.

If you've not attempted to make any kind of costume jewelry before then I highly recommend you use Beadalon that's made up of 19 strands of wire. As well as being pretty flexible it's also very strong.

Material 3 – Cord And Thread

Although most people tend to use wire to make their costume jewelry with, there are plenty of other materials you can use to create some truly spectacular and unique pieces of jewelry.

Elastic Cord

This comes in a number of different thicknesses and colors and is sold by the spool. Although it's the best material to use for making bracelets some people use it to make necklaces for children. As well as it being very versatile it's also very strong. This type of cord tends to be knotted or glued.

Invisible Cord

Also referred to as illusion cord, it 's made from nylon and is very strong. As it is translucent it makes a really amazing addition to any necklace.

Kevlar

Although this particular thread is more commonly used in the creation of bulletproof vests it can prove very useful when making costume jewelry. As it's much more heat resistant, the chances of it stretching is far less. However you need to be aware this particular type of thread is more susceptible to fraying.

Leather Cord

Just as with elastic cord this is available in a variety of different thicknesses and is really suitable for using when making items of jewelry that involve the use of large beads or pendants. To finish off your necklace or bracelet when using leather cords you can either knot it or glue the ends together. However crimping the ends is another way to ensure everything remains in place.

Nymo

This is a waxed nylon thread that comes on small bobbins and is available in various different thicknesses from 00 to FF. 00 Nymo is very fine and as a result can snap very easily, whereas FF is extremely thick and threading beads etc. on to it can prove difficult. When it comes to using this particular type of thread with go for the type that's classified as B or D. This is the perfect thread to use when wanting to weave beads together as it's fine enough to thread the beads on and yet very durable.

Nylon Thread

This is the least expensive type of thread you can buy. I'd recommend you use this only when practicing how to make a particular piece of jewelry you've designed yourself.

Polyester Cord

This is a very durable material and it won't shrink when it comes into contact with moisture. Also you'll find it's less likely to fray as silk will.

Satin Cord

When it comes to using this cord you'll find there's three types to choose from. These are known as Rattail, Mousetail and Bugtail. Each one is a different thickness and all come in a wide variety of different colors and knots. This type of cord is ideal when you're using large beads or wanting to use Chinese knotting methods to create something really unusual.

Silamide

This is a 2 ply twisted nylon thread that's been specifically made for use by those who make clothes by hand. This particular thread is coated in wax but can still be used in the same way as you would use the thread Nymo that we looked at above.

Silk Thread

This is a very versatile type of thread and comes in numerous different colors and thicknesses. The thinnest type of silk thread is numbered 0 whilst the thickest is 16. This particular thread is very easy to knot and is perfect when making costume jewelry that incorporates very delicate beads like pearls in the design. However be aware that this thread will stretch, so you may find stretching it before you begin using it would be a good idea.

Suede Cord

This is much thicker and flatter than leather cord, but is still suitable and is something I would normally use to make chokers or bracelets with. As this material is quite expensive you may want to consider using faux suede instead. Not only is this type of cord cheaper, but also is much stronger than genuine suede and seems to be more consistent in color.

Material 4 – Beads

When it comes to making your own costume jewelry you'll find you're spoilt for choice as to which types of beads to use. Not only do they come in a wide range of sizes, colors and textures but also in a wide variety of shapes. So choosing the right ones can prove quite challenging. Remember the ones you use will determine just how the item looks once completed. Some beads are able make jewelry look quite funky or trendy, whilst others will help add a touch of elegance or sophistication to the piece.

So in order to help you with making a more informed decision about which types of beads to use we briefly take a look at the types below.

Acrylic Beads

These tend to be quite large in size but weigh very little and are perfect to use when making more chunky pieces of jewelry. Use these beads when you want to make a piece of jewelry stands out because these are very bright in color.

Swarovski Beads and Crystals

As well as being the most expensive types of beads you can use for making jewelry with they are the most elegant. They are expensive because it takes time and effort to provide them with so many different faces and to polish them to such a high sheen.

Semi Precious Gemstone Beads

These types of beads tend to be made from jasper, agate, quartz or turquoise and are quite expensive to buy. However they do look absolutely stunning and add a touch of class to any piece of custom jewelry you're making.

Glass Beads

Glass beads are one of the most versatile materials you can use Not only do they look great when included in necklaces or brooches but also in bracelets and earrings. They can be threaded onto wire or sewn on to other materials such as suede, leather or silk.

Metal Beads

Although they look wonderful as the main component in any piece of costume jewelry they work well as spacer beads in a design as well. You can either spend a little more on ones made from gold or silver or you can keep your costs down by going for those made from brass, aluminium or copper.

Seed Beads

These ones work well when you're creating pieces of jewelry that require stitch beadwork within the design. These come in a variety of different shapes from round to square ones. However you'll find when it comes to colors, the choices available are quite limited; most tend to be in neutral shades.

Shamballa Fashion Beads

These types of beads can either be made using clay, which is then covered in crystal or from metal covered in crystal. The clay types are more expensive but are less likely to tarnish over time as the metal based ones will. The great thing about these beads is not only do they add a touch of sparkle to any design but also come in a wide variety of colors.

Wood Beads

Not only are these the cheapest types of beads you can buy for making jewelry but also proves to be the most versatile. These are great for making men's jewelry too. Mixing several different types of wooden beads offers you the opportunity to come up with some very effective but also very simple designs.

Material 5 – Jewelry Clasps

It's important when making costume jewelry you finish each piece off properly and that's why you need to make sure you invest money in buying jewelry clasps. Not only are they an integral part of any piece of jewelry they also help to hide unsightly ends of an item. As you'll discover there are many different types of clasps you can use. Some are quite elegant and others quite whimsical, but all add the finishing touch to your jewelry.

Adjustable Clasp

This is made up of a hook and eye and comes with a small amount of chain attached. Using this type of clasp in a necklace will enable the person wearing it to vary its length when being worn.

Ball And Joint Clasp

In order to keep the clasp closed, pressure needs to be applied to the ball. As these particular clasps are very easy to open and close you should only be using them on necklaces that weigh very little.

Bar And Ring Toggle Clasp

This is in fact a two-piece clasp, where one piece is formed into a loop and the other part is a "T" shaped bar. To close the clasp you need to pull the bar through the loop. They not only come in a variety of different materials but also designs and weights. This type of clasp is most often used on lariat style necklaces or for bracelets or anklets.

Barrel Clasp

Sometimes referred to as the Torpedo clasp, these are low profile ones with threading. To open or close this type of clasp it needs to be twisted.

Bead Clasp

This looks like a bead but is made up of a magnet, tab or bayonet type closure. The wonderful thing about this type of clasp is when closed it blends into the rest of the jewelry so making it look more aesthetically pleasing.

Box Clasp

Also known as the Tab Insert. This clasp is made up of a tab, which inserts into a decorative box or frame. You may find some of these clasps come with safety latches or chains that help to stop the wedge shaped tab from coming out and so prevent the necklace or bracelet falling off the wearer. These can be very decorative and in some cases may be accented with gemstones, inlay work or enamel. Again you would use these types of clasps when making pieces of lightweight jewelry.

Button Toggle Clasp

This is a set of matched buttons where one has a loop of cord attached. To close the clasp in place the loop of cord is placed around the other button.

Crimping Clasp

These need to be crimped on to the end of the wire or cord with a pair of flat nose or crimping pliers. Some of these clasps may include a hook and eye arrangement, whilst others may include a lobster claw or magnetic arrangement.

Filigree Clasp

This type of clasp comes with an open filigree surface that looks similar to lace but of course is made from metal. You may find this type of clasp includes box or fishhook style clasps.

Fishhook Clasp

30

These clasps are small in size and come with a fishhook shaped interior hook that's then inserted into a box oval in shape. The hook inside prevents pieces of jewelry falling off the wearer should the clasp become open accidentally by hooking itself on to the crossbar that's situated within the clasp. You should use this type of clasp when making lightweight pieces of costume jewelry.

Hook And Eye Clasp

Also known as the hook style clasp this is probably the oldest type of clasp for making costume jewelry in use today. This particular type of clasp proves popular as it comes in such a wide range of styles, designs and patterns. This type of clasp is one that's best used when making costume jewelry necklaces or chain belts.

Lobster Claw Clasp

This type of clasp is self-closing and it has been given its particular name because of the general design of it. It's spring-loaded and yet is still available in a wide selection of different styles, shapes and sizes. As it comes in different sizes it can be used on all types of costume jewelry no matter what they weigh.

Magnetic Clasp

This is simply made up of two clasps which contain magnets inside and which help to hold the clasp together. They do help to keep the jewelry secure when being worn, but removing the item is a lot easier and a lot quicker.

Multi Strand Clasp

This type of clasp secures jewelry in place using two, three, four or more strands. To help make these clasps look more elegant some may have gemstones, inlay work or enamel added to them.

S Hook Clasp

This type of clasp is double ended with one being shaped like an "S", whilst the other end is shaped like a ring. To open the clasp you need to pull on the "S" whilst to close the clasp you need to pinch the "S".

Screw Clasp

This particular clasp comes with a threaded screw closure and is similar in design to the barrel type one. However to help camouflage the clasp this one is designed to actually look like a bead.

Slide Lock Clasp

This particular clasp is made up of a set of tubes with one tube sliding into the other and then locking into place. This bar style clasp is made up of multiple strands that allows an unlimited number of chain, cord, beading wire or thread strands to be held in place.

Snap Lock Clasp

Sometimes referred to as the Fold Over Clasp these are low profile clasps, which are far less likely to become entangled in your hair or clothes when being worn. The clasp is hinged and folds shut so securely locking it in place. This particular type of clasp is suitable when making bracelets or anklets.

Open

Closed

Springing Clasp

This type of clasp is used with a jump ring or chain tab in order to make a complete clasp. To open it you pull the trigger, then when it is released it closes automatically. It comes in a number of different sizes and can be used for making costume jewelry that's made up of single or multiple strands.

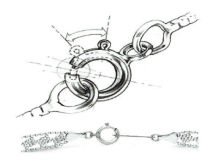

Swivel Clasp

This may look similar in shape to the lobster style clasp but it works in a totally different way. To open and close this clasp you need to twist it through 360 degrees. Although you may want to consider using this clasp when making necklaces you'll find it works best on anklets or bracelets.

Tab Lock Clasp

To close this particular clasp you simply need to insert the decorative tab into the slot that makes up the other half of this clasp. It's held in place by the weight of the jewelry to which it has been attached. As these types of clasps are easy to open and close it's best to use them when making costume jewelry necklaces.

Twister Clasp

This type of clasp is hinged and requires it to be hooked through each end of the piece of jewelry to which it has been attached. This type of clasp is best used when making a twisted choker necklace, an opera length pearl strand or a continuous necklace.

Material 6 – Jewelry Findings

These are crucial when making any type of jewelry as they help to keep items threaded on to the wire or other material in place.

Crimp Tube And Cover

By adding a crimp tube and cover you're creating a more refined and professional finish to your jewelry pieces. These tend to be placed on the ends as they work well as closures.

Jump Ring

This is one of the most important items you should keep a stock of when making jewelry, as they are extremely versatile. They can be used to attach clasps, charms or pendants to your jewelry.

Head Pin And Eye Pin

This is something you'll need from the outset when making costume jewelry as they are important for making all sorts of pieces. Not only do they come in a wide variety of different sizes but also are made from variety of different metals. Plus you may find going for some of the more decorative designs can help you to come up with some truly unique pieces of jewelry.

Bead Tips

These are needed to enable you to join thread to a clasp. Not only are these easy to use but prove very effective in helping to strengthen the ends of the jewelry pieces. I would highly recommend using these when making any costume jewelry from silk.

Jewelry Links

These are suitable for when you need to make a necklace a little longer or where you intend to use more than one strand of threading material in your design. As well as these links coming in a variety of different materials, they also come in a variety of different styles and sizes.

Bails

These allow you to easily attach a pendant to a necklace. Although they may look very simple in design they add a certain touch of class to it. Although these can be made from base metals they can also be made from sterling silver or gold. Not only do they help to provide a more professional finish to your design but will help yours to stand out.

Bead Cap

These caps provide your finished item with a more professional touch that no other component is able to provide. They come in quite simple and elaborate designs so when added will help to make your piece look even more unique.

Cones

This type of jewelry finding can be used to finish off costume jewelry made up of multiple strands or to make tassels for adding to your design. Plus they can also be used as caps on large size beads. There are many different styles of cones available and all can add a more geometric texture to your jewelry designs. They come in a wide array of different materials including copper, silver, gold, pewter or vermeil.

Bead Frame

Adding such to your jewelry designs will help to accent the crystals or beads within the piece more. They come in a wide array of different but very elegant shapes, colors and designs. To attach the frame to the bead you simply string the bead to the center of it. However if you want to create the right look make sure you choose a frame that's the same shape as the head of the bead you are using. You can either use just one-bead frame to highlight one certain bead within your design or you can link several together.

Chapter 3 – Where To Buy Equipment And Materials For Making Costume Jewelry

When it comes to purchasing equipment and materials for making costume jewelry you'll have a number of places to choose from. In this part of the book we not only look at some of the places where the items needed for making such jewelry can be found, but also how to go about purchasing what you need without having to spend too much.

Place 1 – Hobby And Craft Store

These types of places tend to have only a limited amount of jewelry making supplies and equipment. Certainly as these places tend to have most of the basic items and materials needed for making jewelry with, then this would be the best place to start looking for what you need. If you cannot find such a store locally, then search online for one instead.

Place 2 – eBay

You may be wondering why we would suggest eBay but as you'll soon discover there are many great places selling a wide array of materials and equipment for making jewelry with. Yes eBay is a great place for buying what you need at pretty low prices; you still have to be wary about who you purchase from.

It's important you make sure you carry out a few checks into the seller before you make that all important purchase. One of the most important things you need to do is actually read through any feedback left by people who have purchased from them previously. This is the best place to purchase materials and equipment if you're only after small quantities.

Place 3 – Online Jewelry Supply Stores

There's numerous online jewelry supply stores where you can purchase everything you'll need for making costume jewelry with. However as with buying items through eBay it's important you carry out some checks before you make that all important purchase.

One of the things you should be looking at when considering buying online is what sorts of guarantees does the seller offer. A seller who can be relied on will offer some form of money back or replacement guarantee on your purchase if you're not satisfied with the product or if the product is damaged or doesn't work. If the site you're considering buying from doesn't offer one then don't buy from it.

How To Go About Purchasing Material And Equipment For Making Costume Jewelry On A Budget

Not only can making your own jewelry be a great deal of fun, but also can prove a very rewarding hobby as well. However purchasing what you need, can prove quite expensive but below are tips, which can help you to save some money when you first start out.

Tip 1 – When it comes to buying materials for making jewelry with it's best if you purchase wholesale. There are numerous websites to be found that allow you to buy in bulk. To find them, all you need to do is simply type in to Google "wholesale jewelry making supplies" and a list of sites will be made available to you.

Generally what you find with these sites is the more you buy the larger discount you'll be offered. I would highly recommend you use these sites for buying items such as ear wires, clasps and jump rings or any other types of jewelry findings you use regularly. Okay you may have to spend a bit up front but it could save you quite a bit of money in the future.

Tip 2 – When you're going to be buying any equipment or materials for making jewelry online then look for those sites that will ship the goods for free. However be aware many of those stores that offer free shipping tend to ask you to place an order that's worth a certain amount of money, but there are a few that will offer free shipping without any restrictions placed on you. One such site you may want to consider using is Artbeads.com this site offers shipping to its customers for free without needing to place a minimum order amount.

Tip 3 – If you have the opportunity, go visit any jewelry trade shows you hear about in the area where you live. Most of these shows tend to be open to the public as well as trade in the hope they can sell on some of the pieces of jewelry they've designed.

Tip 4 – When it comes to buying materials for making costume jewelry you should think about visiting your local thrift store and purchase pieces of jewelry from them. Then take them home and take them apart and use the components from these items in pieces of jewelry you've designed yourself.

Tip 5 – When you need wire for wire wrapping projects then go to your local hardware store and get what you need. Instead of using silver wire purchase some dark annealed steel wire instead as this is much more durable and will also give your pieces of jewelry a very unique look.

Tip 6 – Before you go out to purchase what you need you should first determine how much you could afford to spend on the materials you need for the coming month or year. By having a budget in place you'll actually prevent yourself from spending more than you can afford to.

Types Of Costume Jewelry

A lot of people are put off wearing costume jewelry because they see it as being cheap and tacky and made from only the cheapest materials possible. Yet it may surprised you and them to learn there are certain pieces of costume jewelry that are just as valuable as real pieces of jewelry as they have been created by some very famous designers.

This particular type of jewelry is to be worn as part of the latest fashions.

Type 1 – Vintage Costume Jewelry

This is the type of costume jewelry was made during a certain style era. For example, pieces made during the latter part of the 1800's would be classed as being Victorian vintage costume jewelry. Whereas pieces made during the 1920's and 1930's would be classed as art deco pieces.

Certainly the styles of vintage costume jewelry are proving most popular today and which you can create your own designs similar to them are those from the Victorian, Edwardian and Art Deco periods. If at all possible you'll need to use materials that have an aged look about them or are actually from pieces of jewelry that came from those periods in time. The best place to search for what you need often tends to be in antique stores.

Type 2 – Reproduction Costume Jewelry

This particular type of costume jewelry is actually designed to look like it's come from a certain period in time, but has in fact been made using materials available today. What you'll find is these items of costume jewelry tend to be exact copies of designs, which originally came about during the period they relate to.

If you use the finest quality materials available you may find people have difficulties in telling the piece you've created isn't the genuine article.

Type 3 – Normal Costume Jewelry

This is the type of jewelry you'll find little girls enjoy wearing when dressing up. Typically made from plastic these are very quick and easy to make and will add a splash of color to any outfit. The style of this type of costume jewelry tends to be largely based on the kind of jewelry women wore during the 1920's and 1930's.

Chapter 4 – Tips To Get Started Making Costume Jewelry

Before you even think about purchasing any materials for making costume jewelry, you first need to decide what sort of jewelry you wish to make. Do you want to make just necklaces, earrings or bracelets or do you want to make them all? Yes you can make them all, however it would be far better if you decide on one particular piece of jewelry and then work on this alone.

You should only buy the materials you need when you know what jewelry you're going to make. What materials you use of course will be dependent on what you can afford to spend. Although you may be tempted to try and make several pieces at a time it's far better to actually focus on just making one piece at a time to ensure the quality of the piece is the highest possible.

When it comes to buying materials, whether it's from your local supply store or online you may find it hard to resist buying everything that's available. But be careful, as you don't want to end up like so many others who have spent hundreds of dollars buying materials they never use. In the beginning it's best to start out by making some very simple pieces, then as your confidence and skills grow move on to making more elaborate pieces of costume jewelry.

Also before you do go out and buy materials don't forget to consider where the work is being done. This will help you then decide what sort of storage units you're going to need to keep all your supplies in. Personally I use a set of plastic craft draws in which I keep all my supplies. Not only are the materials easy to reach but also allows me to keep them in order and divide up each material in to a separate compartment. Another thing I also invested in was a bead box, which allows me to keep these items segregated into various sizes.

If you have a room specifically set aside for making costume jewelry in then you can create your own storage units. However if you'll be working on your pieces of jewelry at the kitchen table then keeping all the items together in one unit that can be moved around would be ideal. Plus having everything stored in one place means you can easily find things and you can concentrate more on creating some truly amazing pieces of costume jewelry rather than having to worry about searching for things half way through the project.

One of the most important things you need to remember when making costume jewelry is to have fun. If you find you don't like working with very small pieces such as tiny beads for making earrings then don't. Instead work on using much larger beads only.

It's important you do a little research before you start buying materials. Then when you have finished creating your pieces don't be surprised if you have people asking where you bought yours from.

The other thing you should also do before you actually start trying to make your own pieces of costume jewelry is to start honing certain skills needed. I would highly recommend you spend time honing the various wiring techniques you'll often need to use to create some very visually exciting pieces of jewelry. Spending a couple of weeks on learning and practicing such skills can really make a huge difference to how your finished product looks.

When making any kind of jewelry it's best to use the least expensive materials initially. Then if a mistake is made you won't feel so upset about the money you've wasted.

Here's some other advice for making jewelry:

Finding Inspiration For Making Costume Jewelry

If you don't know where to begin then there are plenty of ways to come up with some ideas to help you get started.

As well as looking around you for inspiration, there are numerous websites that actually provide you with ideas as well. When trying to come up with ideas there are a few things to do.

1. Create a folder or scrapbook into which ideas for creating your own costume jewelry can be placed. Take your ideas from magazines and catalogues. However rather than making pieces look similar to those you have seen, instead draw on various aspects of the pieces you like and create something that's totally unique.

2. Look at things in nature. Look at leafs and flowers to conjure up designs you can then create amazing pieces of costume jewelry from. You'll be amazed at just how many different shapes there are that'll help you to create some truly spectacular pieces. You don't even need to leave your home to find inspiration, simply look out of a window and see what's there.

3. If things in nature don't provide you with the necessary inspiration then look at other shapes around you. Simple squares, circles and triangles can really help you to come up with some amazing designs as well.

4. Although we recommend you use beads etc. in your designs don't be afraid to experiment making costume jewelry with other materials. Using polyclay or acrylic resin could prove wonderful. The great thing about using polyclay is you're able to create your own shapes. Then once you've created the shapes you like, you simply bake it in the oven before adding it into your piece of costume jewelry. However,

don't forget to include a hole or a small piece on to which a cap can be fitted.

5. Look closely at pieces of vintage costume jewelry. The main periods in our history when this form of jewelry was fashionable was during 1900 and 1918 known as the Edwardian Period an 1919 to 1929 the Art Deco period. Also look at jewelry made between 1930 and 1939 when the Great Depression was taking place. As you will discover the designs at this time were extremely varied and the materials used in creating pieces of costume jewelry at this time was also extremely varied.

6. As already mentioned above take a jewelry course if you can locally. However if you're finding it difficult to find such courses locally there are plenty of online ones you can participate in instead.

When it comes to choosing such a course make sure the following is included.

a) It covers the techniques to help you design and create your own mood board.

b) It provides you with advice and information about how to extract inspiration from a large array of sources, as well as helping you to add these into the pieces you create.

c) The course should teach you how to use a wide range of different materials for making costume jewelry with.

d) Look for courses that are run by people with plenty of experience in making all forms of jewelry, but especially the costume type.

e) Finally look for courses where classes are kept to only a small number of students. This will help to ensure you get the most out of the course as well as providing you with more personal tutoring. A course that allows only 8 students is ideal.

By getting involved in such courses it offers you not only the opportunity to take up a hobby you'll find extremely interesting but could lead you to creating a business that may help to bring in an additional income.

Tips To Help With Making Costume Jewelry A Lot Easier

1. It is a good idea if you tie knots between each bead or other item you include within your piece as this will help to reduce the need for you to have to restring the entire piece should the thread or wire break.

2. It is important you handle the beads in your pieces very carefully as they can often be quite delicate and so are likely to become scratched or they could break.

3. Before you attempt to come up and then create your own designs it's a good idea to practice what you've learnt by following some costume jewelry patterns that can be found online. Including the ones that are offered in the next chapter of this book.

4. When it comes to cutting the string or wire for your costume jewelry make sure you cut it a few inches longer to what you think you'll be need. If you don't then adding additional string or wire to your piece is difficult and won't give you the professional finish you're after.

5. Make sure you vary not only the size and color of the beads but also the shape. This will help to make your designs look more unique and interesting.

6. Never leave any loose beads lying around especially if you have small children. Not only can these become easily lost

but also there's every possibility your child may eat them thinking they're sweets.

Chapter 5 – Some Projects For Making Costume Jewelry You May Want To Try

Before I give you some projects to try out yourself. There are certain things you need to do first before you begin.

One of the most important things you must do is find a good place to buy your jewelry supplies through. Although you may have suppliers locally I would recommend you don't limit yourself to using just them but also use various suppliers online who tend to go under the title of "bead shops" or "jewelry supplies".

There are certain benefits to be had from buying your costume jewelry supplies online. One of these being they tend to have a wider selection of materials available. Also you may find that because you buy bulk amounts of various items they'll give you a discount.

The second most important thing to do is source the best quality materials and tools you can afford. The problem with buying online is you have to rely on the pictures they published on a website and unfortunately there are some unscrupulous people around who will publish pictures of items that are nothing like they're selling.

When buying online make sure you read through any description of the items provided and if unsure about your purchase don't be afraid to ask the seller for more information. If they are unwilling or cannot provide you with further information then look elsewhere. Also don't forget to look to see what sort of guarantee the seller offers. If no guarantees are provided then look elsewhere.

Finally it's important you create a list of the supplies needed to make a specific piece of jewelry. Then look through various catalogs and sites to see what's available and work out how much everything will cost. This also means you have the opportunity to compare prices of various items and get the best deals possible whilst not having to compromise on quality.

Project 1 – Lampwork Bracelet

It's quite possible for you to make a beautiful costume lampwork bracelet simply by using beads that are a different size, color and type to those in this tutorial.

Supplies Required To Make Lampwork Bracelet

1. 19 Strand Beadalon Wire
2. Lampwork Beads or Any Other Beads You Wish To Use
3. 2 x Toggle Clasps
4. 2 x 5-6mm Jump Rings
5. 2 x Calottes
6. Blue Crystal Beads (Optional – You Can Use Swarovski ones)
7. Bali Spacer Beads (Optional)
8. Crimp Beads
9. Crimping Pliers
10. Chain Nose Pliers
11. Wire or Side Cutters

Step 1 – You need to first cut a piece of the 19-strand Beadalon wire that's 1 inch longer than the actual bracelet length. Once you've cut the right length of wire, on one end of the string put a crimp bead and then with the crimping pliers compress the bead into a ball.

Step 2 – Next thread on to the wire a calotte, making sure the crimp bead is sat in the middle of it. Then cut off any excess wire next to the bead so that nothing will be sticking out.

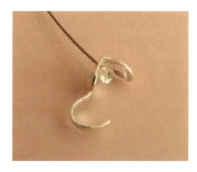

Step 3 – You need to very gently close the calotte with your flat nose or chain nose pliers until it is shut completely (As per the picture below).

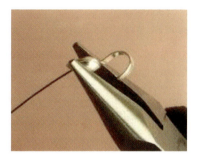

Step 4 – Now open the loop on the calotte with your chain nose pliers and into this insert the jump ring. Once you have inserted the jump ring you must remember to close the calotte loop.

Step 5 – Next you need to open the jump ring. You do this by holding it on each side with a pair of chain nose and round nose pliers and pull each side away from the other. Once a large enough gap has been made between the jump rings two ends, insert the bar of the toggle clasp on to it. Then close the jump ring by pushing each side towards the other.

Step 6 – After adding the toggle clasp you can now start threading the beads on to your bracelet. Begin by threading on a crystal bead before then threading on a lampwork bead. Then follow this again with a crystal bead, then thread on one of the bali beads before then starting again with a crystal bead followed by a lampwork bead. Of course you don't need to thread the beads on in this order, you can actually thread them in any order you like.

Step 7 – Once you've finished threading the beads on to the wire you must now attach another crimp bead, jump ring, calotte and toggle clasp on. Be careful when adding the calottes on to the bracelet as they're very delicate and break easily.

Step 8 – Finally before you close the shells on the calotte cut off any excess wire with your side or wire cutters. Once the calotte has been attached open up the loop on it and insert the jump ring then close the loop up again.

Step 9 – Next open the jump ring as already described above and insert the toggle clasp ring. Once you've closed the jump ring back up the bracelet is now ready to wear.

Project 2 – Amethyst Link Bracelet

This particular project consists of wire wrapped amethyst beads that are joined together using jump rings. The great thing about this project is there are only two techniques you need to have mastered in order to create this wonderful piece of costume jewelry.

To make my bracelet I have chosen to use 5mm twisted and 9mm open jump rings as the links between each of the beads. However you don't need to use amethyst beads in your bracelet you can in fact use any beads you like, as they'll look just as great.

Supplies Required To Make Amethyst Link Bracelet

1. 3 or 4 Amethyst Beads (Or Any Beads You Like)
2. 4 to 6 Twisted 5mm Jump Rings
3. 8 to 10 Open 9mm Jump Rings (Use the thickest jump rings possible)
4. 6 to 8 Flower Spacer Beads
5. Clasp and Hook
6. 18g (1.0mm) or 20g (0.8mm) Wire (What size you use will depend on the size of the holes that have been drilled into the beads you are using)
7. Pair Round Nose Pliers
8. Pair of Chain or Flat Nose Pliers
9. Pair of Wire or Side Cutters
10. Pair of Safety Goggles (Glasses) (Optional)

Step 1 – The first thing you need to do is make the wrapped bead links by joining the beads and spacer beads together. To make the wrapped bead links you cut around 3 to 4 inches of the wire off and then slide the bead on to the middle of this piece. Now grip one end of the wire about 5mm above the bead with the round nose pliers and bend the wire to form a 90 degree angle by moving the pliers away from you.

Then with your free hand bend the tip of this wire clockwise around the nose of the pliers. You may find that you need to reposition the pliers once or twice whilst doing this. Keep bending the wire until a complete loop is formed now release the pliers.

Now add the bead link using your free hand to wrap the wire at least 2.5 to 3 times around the neck of the loop to ensure it's held in place. Any excess wire should be cut off and the end of it pressed down with the chain nose pliers. Repeat this process at the other end of the wire so you end up with the finished product shown in the picture below.

Step 2 – You now need to open one of the 9mm jump rings by holding either side with a pair of round nose pliers and the flat or chain nose pliers and pull them away from each other. Once you've opened the space between the two ends of the jump ring enough slide on to it one of the 6mm twisted jump rings on to the 9mm jump ring. Now take a second 9mm jump ring and open this up and slide the twisted jump bead through the space made. Then slide on to this jump ring one of the wrapped link beads you made earlier. Now you're able to close the jump ring up completely by pushing both sides back towards the other. Please be careful when opening and closing the jump rings because if you pull or push on them too hard they can break easily.

Step 3 – Now do the same again using the rest of the bead links and jump rings. How many bead links you use will depend on the size of bracelet you are making, which of course depends on the size of the wrist of the person who will be wearing the completed piece.

Step 4 – Once you have added the final jump ring link you need to attach the clasp and hook. To do this you must open the last jump ring added on to both ends of the bracelet and onto one you thread the clasp and on to the other you thread the hook. After threading the clasp and hook on make sure that you close each jump ring completely. Now the bracelet is ready to be worn.

Project 3 – Watermelon Tourmaline Bracelet

Not only is this stunning to look at but making costume jewelry like this is very easy. It can be worn both with formal and more casual outfits in your wardrobe or in your friends wardrobes if they ask you to make it for them.

As already mentioned making it is very simple, the challenge for you comes when deciding what types of gemstones to incorporate into your design. Of course to add a little glitz and glamour to the design incorporate a few silver nuggets between some of the gems you choose to include in your design.

Supplies Needed For Making Watermelon Tourmaline Bracelet

1. 15 Different Colored Tourmaline Stones
2. 1 Rose Color Watermelon Tourmaline Stone
3. 1 .925 Silver Toggle
4. 2 Silver Crimps
5. 26 to 28 Silver Nuggets
6. Bead Wire Measuring 17 Inches
7. Pair of Round Nose Pliers
8. Pair of Chain Nose or Flat Nose Pliers
9. Pair of Crimp Pliers
10. Pair of Wire or Side Cutters
11. Safety Glasses (Optional)

Step 1 – Fold the bead wire in half and then insert the loop created into the toggle and pull tight.

Step 2 – Now take one of the silver crimps and slide this on to the bead wire until it is right beside the toggle and with the crimping pliers close the crimp up.

Step 3 – Next take two of the silver nuggets and thread these onto the bead wire followed by the tourmaline stone and then follow this by another silver nugget. Continue to do this until all the tourmaline stones and silver nuggets have been used up.

Step 4 - Once the last tourmaline stone has been threaded on then thread on the rest of the silver nuggets. By now the bracelet should measure at least 7 inches long with the toggle included. If it's not then thread some more silver nuggets on to the wire.

Step 5 – As soon as the bracelet is the right length, thread on the second crimp bead and insert the wire through hole that's on the other part of the toggle. Then thread this back through the crimp bead and pull tight. Now take your crimp pliers and shut the crimp tightly. Rather than cutting any excess wire off simply tuck it back through the silver nuggets.

Project 4 – Chain Drop Earrings

This'll go perfectly with any outfit being worn for a special evening out. They don't take very long to make and you can decide just how long or short these should be whilst making costume jewelry like this.

Supplies Needed For Making Chain Drop Earrings

1. 2 Small and 2 Medium Size Crystal Beads
2. 2 Bali Flower Spacer Beads
3. 2 Headpins
4. Piece of Chain That Contains No Less Than 20 Links
5. 2 Fish Hook Earring Wires
6. 2 (2mm or 3mm) Jump Rings
7. Pair Round Nose Pliers
8. Pair of Wire Or Side Cutters
9. Safety Glasses (Optional)

NB: PLEASE MAKE SURE YOU MAKE EACH EARRING AT THE SAME TIME FOLLOWING THE STEP BY STEP GUIDE PROVIDED BELOW. THIS WILL THEN HELP TO ENSURE EACH EARRING IS THE SAME LENGTH.

Step 1 – The first thing you need to do is slide the beads on to the headpin. Begin by sliding on one of the large beads, followed by the ball spacer bead, followed by one of the medium sized beads.

Step 2 – Now you need to make a loop on the headpin. To do this grip the wire to close the bead as you possibly can with your round nose pliers and then with your free hand clockwise wrap some of the excess wire around the prongs of your pliers.

Step 3 – Now you need to cut the chain into two pieces. It is important when doing this you make sure each piece of chain has a total of 10 links.

Step 4 – Now you need to open up the loop you've made on your headpin very slightly. It should just be enough to allow you to slip the first link of the chain on to it. If you open the loop too wide then its round shape will become distorted. Once the chain has been thread on to the loop you can very gently close it up again.

Step 5 – Next take the jump ring and grip each end of it between the round nose and chain nose pliers and open it up by very gently moving the pliers in opposite directions. One set of pliers should be moved forwards whilst the other set are moved backwards. Do not move the pliers left or right, as this will weaken the jump ring. Once you've sufficient space between the two ends of the jump ring you can thread the last link of the chain on to it.

Step 6 – Before you close the jump ring up again to keep everything securely in place you should now also slip the earring wire on to it. When it comes to closing the jump ring make sure you do so in the same way it was opened. Also it's important to make sure the jump ring is completely closed.

Project 5 – Winter White Pearl & Glass Earrings

This chandelier style set of earrings looks wonderful worn with any formal outfit especially a little black dress.

Supplies Needed To Make Winter White Pearl & Glass Earrings

1. 2 x 6mm Fire Polished Crystal Matte Glass Beads
2. 4 x 5.5 to 6mm White Button Pearl Beads
3. 2 x Ring Round Chandelier Components
4. 2 x Sterling Silver Ear Hooks
5. 6 x Sterling Silver Head Pins
6. Pair Round Nose Pliers
7. Pair Chain Nose or Flat Nose Pliers
8. Pair Wire or Side Cutters
9. Pair Safety Glasses (Optional)

Step 1 – Take one of the pearl beads and thread on to a head pin and then make a loop at one end of the head pin. Now cut off an excess head pin wire and repeat the same process with the rest of the pearl beads and the matte glass beads.

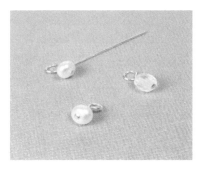

Step 2 – Now slip the loop of one pear on the outside ring of one of the chandelier components. Now on to the next chandelier ring, slip one of the matte glass beads on its loop. Then on the next ring along slip another one of the pear beads. Do the same with the other round chandelier component with the other two pearl beads and the other matte glass bead.

Step 3 – Now to finish the earrings off you simply have to hook the earring hook through the top of each chandelier and they're ready to be worn.

Project 6 – Chunky Lava Bread Wire Wrapped Pendant & Chain

Attaching a large wooden bead can soon become something extra special by adding some wire wrapping into the design. You can either use the wire wrapped bead in a very simple design by threading it on to a chain or you can create something more elaborate by making it the focal point on a necklace that's been strung with beads. This project is the latter one.

Supplies Needed For Making Chunky Lava Bread Wire Wrapped Pendant & Chain

1. 1 x 18 Inch Gold Plated Serpentine Chain

2. 1 x 25mm Puffed Square Brown Lava Bead
3. 12 Inches 21g (0.7mm) Dead Soft Brass or Gold Filled Wire
4. 2 x 4mm Goldstone Beads
5. Pair of Wire or Side Cutters
6. Pair of Chain Nose or Flat Nose Pliers
7. Pair of Round Nose Pliers
8. Pair of Nylon Nosed Pliers
9. Jeweler's File

Step 1 - Make a wire coil on the end of the 12-inch piece of wire using the same techniques for making a wire coil head pin.

Step 2 – Now on the wire, thread one of the goldstone beads followed by the lava bead and then another goldstone bead. Make sure you push them all the way down the wire so the first bead lies flush against the wire coil you've just made.

Step 3 - Now create a wrapped loop around the last bead you added on to the wire and then continue to wrap it around the goldstone bead and down it, as per the picture below.

Step 4 – Next bring the wire down and across one side of the lava bead and then wrap it around the bottom of the lava bead so the wire is wrapped between it and the other goldstone bead.

Step 5 – Then bring the wire back up and across the other side of the lava bead and wrap it around the top again. Make sure you wrap the wire around between the lava bead and the goldstone bead. You should continue to wrap the wire around the top a few times before trimming any excess wire off. Once you've cut off any excess wire. To make it smooth use the jeweller's file to smooth the end of the wire.

Step 6 – Now take your chain nose or flat nose pliers and grasp the wire that's been wrapped across one side of the lava bead and slightly twist it so a small bend has been made into it. However do this very carefully as the wire is quite fragile and if you exert too much pressure it can easily snap and you'll have to start from scratch. Then do the same again on the other side of the lava bead.

Step 7 - Finally all you need to do is slip the lava bead and goldstone bead pendant on to the chain and it is ready to wear.

71

Project 7 – Chunky Funky Heart Necklace

This necklace will take a little longer to make than others in this book. However the finished item looks wonderful and will have your friends clamouring for you to make them one as well.

Supplies Needed To Make The Chunky Funky Heart Necklace

1. Selection of Size 11 Seed Beads In Earth Colors (such as creams, metallic browns and burgundy)
2. Around 20 Inches of Garnet Chip Beads
3. 1 Diamond Shaped Moonstone Bead
4. 4 x 6mm Limestone Beads
5. 12 x Chunky Turquoise Beads
6. 12 x 8mm Leopard Skin Jasper Beads
7. 26 x 6mm Leopard Skin Jasper Beads
8. 12 x 4mm Goldstone Beads
9. 12 x 4mm Tiger's Eye Beads
10. 5 x 4mm Root Bear Colored Czech Beads
11. Heart Pendant

12. 12 Inches of 20g (0.8mm) Sterling Wire
13. 6 Crimp Beads
14. Approximately 3ft of .014 Beading Wire
15. Approximately 6inches of Beading Thread
16. 1 Beading Needle
17. Pair of Crimping Pliers
18. Pair of Scissors
19. Pair of Round Nose Pliers
20. Pair of Wire or Side Cutters
21. A Shallow Bowl

If you're having problems sourcing the beads mentioned above locally then you may want to consider purchasing what you need online instead.

Step 1 - Begin by threading three separate strands of beads on to the beading wire. Start off by threading up to 20 inches of the garnet chips on to the beading wire and then finishing off with a crimp bead.

Step 2 – On to the next strand thread some of the chunky beads. Start off with one of the chunky turquoise beads, then thread on to this one of the 6mm leopard skin beads followed by one of the 4mm goldstone beads and then follow this with one of the 8mm leopard skin beads.

Follow this with a goldstone bead before threading on another 6mm leopard skin bead, a chunky turquoise bead and another 6mm leopard skin bead. Then thread on one of the 4mm Tiger's eye beads followed by the 8mm leopard skin beads, another 4mm Tiger's eye bead and another one of the leopard skin jasper beads.

Continue doing this until a total of 20 inches of beads have been threaded on to the beading wire. Again finish off the threading with a crimp bead.

Step 3 – On the third strand of beading wire you're going to be threading the various colored seed beads. However these don't need to go on in any particular order. Simply place the seed beads in the shallow dish and mix them around and then string them on the beading wire. The best way of doing this is to simply poke the beading wire into the bowl and then scoop up one of the beads on to it.

After you have threaded on a few inches of these beads, now add on to it one of the 6mm limestone beads, one of the leopard skin jasper beads, one of the Czech beads and finally a moonstone bead. Then start scooping more of the seed beads on to the beading wire adding as mentioned above every few inches until once again you've made a necklace that's 20 inches long. Just as with the other parts of this necklace finish off the piece with a crimp bead.

Step 4 – Take the sterling wire and make a triple flower loop. Before you actually close up each loop, thread on to each one of the ends the beaded strands you have made earlier. Ensure they rest in two of the three loops created.

Step 5 – Now make a very simple hook with the sterling wire and connect this to the third loop in the triple flower loop made earlier.

Step 6 – Next take some more of the sterling wire and again make another flower loop, however this one will have four loops rather than three and the final loop needs to be wrapped closed.

Step 7 – Now with the other sides of the necklaces, you snake each end of them through three of the loops.

Step 8 – Take some beading thread and the needle and on thread some of the seed beads you used earlier to make a bail for the heart pendant.

To connect each end of the thread, use a few overhead knots and thread back onto the beads. The bail itself should be about 1.5 inches long as this will then make it much easier to slip over the three strands that make up the rest of this necklace.

Project 8 – Kokopelli Pendant With Glass & Turquoise Beads Necklace

You can string together not only turquoise and clear colored glass beads to form this necklace but any colors you wish. Although I've chosen to use a Native American inspired copper Kokopelli pendant in this project you can use any style of Kokopelli pendant you want. Just make sure the pendant you select is one that complements or matches the other beads you've chosen to create this costume jewelry necklace with.

Supplies You Need For Making Kokopelli Pendant With Glass & Turquoise Beads

1. Copper Clay Kokopelli Pendant
2. 3 x 3mm Copper Daisy Spacer Beads
3. 1 Copper Lobster Claw Clasp
4. 1 Inch of 21g (0.7mm) Dead Soft Copper Wire
5. 1 x 3mm Copper Jump Ring
6. 2 x 2mm Crimp Beads
7. Selection of Turquoise and Clear Glass Beads
8. Bead Bowl (As you will be threading the beads on to the wire in a random fashion having a bead bowl to keep the beads in, as you work can prove useful. However if you don't have a bead bowl any shallow bowl will work just as effectively)
9. Ruler (Measuring Stick)
10. 24 Inches of .019mm Copper Colored Beading Wire
11. 1 x Bead Stopper
12. Pair of Crimping Pliers
13. Pair of Wire or Side Cutters
14. Pair of Chain Nose or Flat Nose Pliers
15. Pair of Round Nose Pliers

Step 1 - The first thing you need to do is add a jump ring to your pendant.

Step 2 – After you've added the jump ring to the pendant you can now begin threading the beads on the beading wire. Start off by threading a bead stopper on to one end of the beading wire and then start to randomly thread on the beads you've placed in the bowl. After adding a few inches of beads on to the wire then think about adding a copper daisy bead on before you thread any more beads on.

Step 3 – After adding at least 9 inches of beads on to the wire you can now thread the pendant on. Make sure you set each strand beside the other to ensure they are all the same length and your pendant is in the middle of the necklace. It's important you do this before you complete the necklace because of the mix of beads you're using.

Step 4 – Now secure one end of your necklace using a crimp bead, making sure you add the lobster claw clasp to the beading wire just before you insert it back into the crimp bead and close it.

Step 5 – Now take a small piece of the copper wire and with the round nose pliers make a "Figure of 8" and repeat step 4 above, but this time only attaching the "Figure of 8" component to the necklace before you thread the wire back through the crimp bead and close it. It's this component that allow you to keep the necklace in place by allowing it to be threaded on to the Lobster Claw Clasp.

Step 6 – Now cut off any excess wire and the necklace is ready to wear.